Dinosaurs

by Annabelle Lynch

W
FRANKLIN WATTS
LONDON•SYDNEY

First published in 2013 by
Franklin Watts
338 Euston Road
London
NW1 3BH

Franklin Watts Australia
Level 17/207 Kent Street
Sydney
NSW 2000

Copyright © Franklin Watts 2013

Picture credits: Linda Bucklin/Shutterstock: 5, 12.
leonello calveni/Shutterstock: 10. Marcel Clemns/
Shutterstock: 19.Mike Danton/Alamy: 6.
Image Source/Corbis: 21. Andreas Meyer/
Shutterstock: 15. Tsuneo MP/Shutterstock: 9.
Jianying Yin/Istockphoto: front cover.

Every attempt has been made to clear copyright.
Should there be any inadvertent omission please
apply to the publisher for rectification.

Dewey number: 567.9

ISBN 978 1 4451 1642 6 (hbk)
ISBN 978 1 4451 1648 8 (pbk)

Series Editor: Julia Bird
Picture Researcher: Diana Morris
Series Advisor: Catherine Glavina
Series Designer: Peter Scoulding

Printed in China

Franklin Watts is a division of Hachette Children's Books,
an Hachette UK company.
www.hachette.co.uk

Contents

The words in **bold** can be found in the glossary.

What were dinosaurs?

Dinosaurs were animals that lived on Earth millions of years ago. Some dinosaurs were very big. Some were very small!

Dinosaur means terrible lizard.

Plant eaters

Some dinosaurs only ate plants. They had long necks, so they could reach up high and down low to find food.

Plant-eating dinosaurs were called herbivores.

Meat eaters

Some dinosaurs only ate meat. They were called carnivores.

The Tyrannosaurus rex had sharp teeth and claws to catch its **prey**.

Armoured dinosaurs

Lots of dinosaurs had horns, spikes and very hard plates called armour. These **protected** them.

Ankylosaurus had horns, spikes on its back and armour on its body.

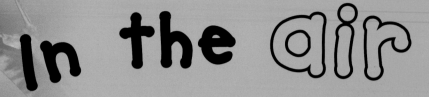

In the air

Huge **reptiles** called pterosaurs lived at the same time as the dinosaurs. They had wings so they could fly.

13

Pterosaurs had **crests** and long beaks.

Under the sea

Sea reptiles called plesiosaurs also lived at the same time as the dinosaurs. They had flippers, which helped them swim fast.

Elasmosaurus had a long, bendy neck.

Crazy dinosaurs

Some dinosaurs looked very strange. Parasaurolophus had a long, **hollow** crest on its head and a beak like a duck.

Parasaurolophus could use its crest to make noises.

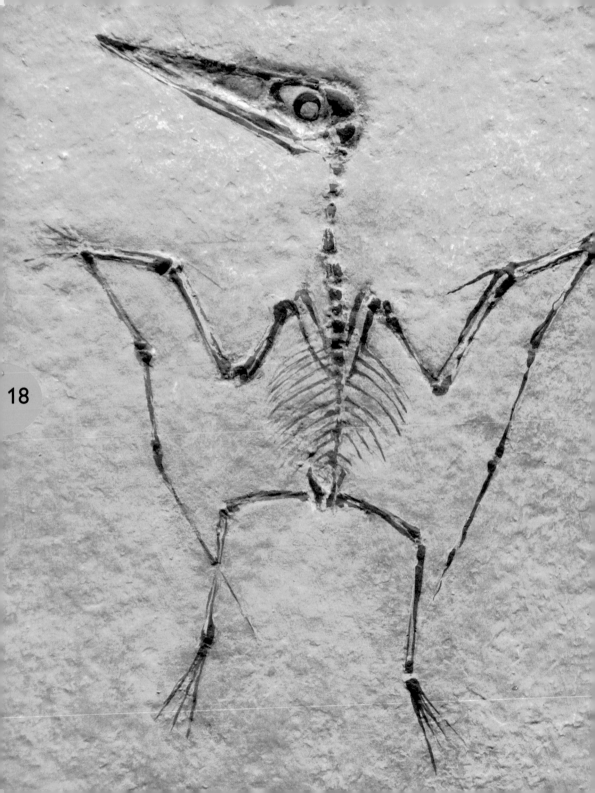

18

How do we know?

Fossils help us find out about dinosaurs. These are the marks that animals and plants leave behind in rocks.

This is the fossil of a pterosaur (see page 13).

Find out!

You can learn about dinosaurs at lots of places, including **museums**. Why not visit one today?

Get up close to a dinosaur!

Glossary

Crest - a ridge of skin or feathers

Hollow - something that is empty inside

Museum - a place where you can see interesting things

Prey - an animal that is eaten by another animal

Reptile - an animal that has scales and lays eggs

Protect - to keep safe

Websites:

http://www.nhm.ac.uk/kids-only/dinosaurs/

http://www. bbc.co.uk/nature/14343366

Every effort has been made by the Publishers to ensure that the websites are suitable for children, and that they contain no inappropriate or offensive material. However, because of the nature of the Internet, it is impossible to guarantee that the contents of these sites will not be altered. We strongly advise that Internet access is supervised by a responsible adult.

Quiz

Use the information in the book to answer these questions.

1. How long ago did dinosaurs live?

2. Which dinosaurs only ate plants?

3. What did ankylosaurus have on its back?

4. What could a parasaurolophus use its crest to do?

5. What are fossils?

6. Where could you go to find out about dinosaurs?

(The answers are on page 24.)

Answers

1. Millions of years ago
2. Herbivores
3. Spikes
4. To make noises
5. The marks that animals and plants leave behind in rocks
6. To a museum

Index